SUNSHINE

WITH SOME DRIZZLE

By

Dr. Charleszetta Stalling

"Eye of the Corner", "It's in the Blood", "Edgar" originally published in *Therefore, We Write*, 2012
"Fire Away" originally published in *Cosumnes River Journal*, 2008

Printed in the United States of America.

I Street Press
828 I Street
Sacramento, CA 95814

****

Stalling, Charleszetta
        Sunshine With Some Drizzle; written and photographed by
        Dr. Charleszetta Stalling
        88 p., 15 cm.

ISBN: 978-0-9913062-7-5

1. Personal Reflections. 2. Poetry. 3. Encouragements.

Library of Congress Control Number: 2014902829

Cover Design by Dr. Charleszetta Stalling

All other designs and photos were taken on location by Dr. Charleszetta Stalling

DEDICATION

This collection of stories, reflections and glimpses is dedicated to the Jackson clan: my grandparents James and Lula Mae Branch; my mother, Ruth Johnny May and the many uncles, aunts and cousins of the family; Simpkins family: my sons, Gary and Ronald; grandsons, Mathew, Gary Jr., Keith, Bryce, and Semaj; brother in law Renee, Frank and his wife, Betty; Stalling family: especially my father, Luther Cecil, brother James and niece Giavanna; plus many friends, neighbors and numerous organizations.

A special acknowledgement is given to Gerry Ward of I Street Press for his time, expertise and dedication to making this publication a reality.

FORWARD

Dr. Charleszetta Stalling is an educator, consultant, trainer and a consummate storyteller. "Sunshine And Some Drizzle," while not an autobiography, the sequence of chapters chronicles her life and living experiences. Her book begins with Chapter I: Love Lost and Found; Chapter II: Jackson Stories Stretched; Chapter III: Ugandan Glimpses; Chapter IV: Growing Up/Childhood Experiences; Chapter V: Growing Pains/Reflections; and ending with Chapter VI: Almost Grown/Mature Reflections.

In 2002, I met Dr. Charleszetta Stalling, in my position as the Director of the Center for African Peace and Conflict Resolution at California State University, Sacramento. She applied and was accepted for the prestigious US Fulbright Hays Group Study Abroad to Uganda, East Africa for five weeks, a professional development program for educators. Her goal was to capture the culture through the written word—short stories, poetry and the oral tradition of storytelling. Refer to Chapter III, Ugandan Glimpses.

Vividly, I remember a cohesive story she created that included the characteristics and behaviors of the 15 Fulbright candidates, my co-director and me. It was insightful yet very funny.

Between each chapter, Dr. Stalling has included pictures of flowers she loves to grow, arrange and photograph.

In summary, Dr. Stalling is a life-long learner, collector of antiques, world traveler, and a person who loves to live life to the fullest with family, friends and colleagues. I hope each reader of this collection feels the sunshine and some drizzle, whether in sunny Kampala, Uganda or in the river city of Sacramento California.

Peace,

Ernest Uwazie, Ph.D.

TABLE OF CONTENTS

I. LOVE LOST AND FOUND   PAGE

II. JACKSON STORIES STRETCHED

III. UGANDAN GLIMPSES

IV. GROWING UP - CHILDHOOD EXPERIENCES

V. GROWING PAINS - REFLECTIONS

VI. ALMOST GROWN - MATURE REFLECTIONS

I. LOVE LOST AND FOUND

CAUGHT IN THE MOMENT OF LOVE

The phone rang a special ring. She felt it was her man. It was her baby!

She smiled upon hearing his melodic, juicy, sweet voice. Her heart jumped with joy and raced with excitement. Yet, she tried to appear calm and collected in front of several girlfriends. We tried not to listen as we did.

He spoke to her of good times, memories, and words of love. Each knew that their intimate relationship would bind and create a circle of love no matter how far away.

Her receptive ears waited, listened and heard as her mind and body responded silently. She looked down at her toes. "I can't. I have company," she shared. Then there was a pause.

"Sunshine With Some Drizzle"
  Dr. Charleszetta Stalling

~ 1 ~

"Yes, toes," she softly cooed. We tried not to listen as we did.

She thought, "Baby, I want to be your greens, black eyed-peas, cornbread, chitterlings so good that they are chitlins, tender roasted duck, juicy turkey wings, dirty rice hot with pepper and ground beef as you like, deviled eggs and sweet, sweet potato pie with nutmeg. Devour me for I want to be all that's good to you. I adore you, love you, always, more and more. Hunger and thirst for me as I do you."

The conversation was coming to a quick end. She had company. She smiled, satisfied for the moment. She too, could hardly wait for them to be together again.

She admired the succulent, good smelling food she had lovingly prepared for him though he was 5000 miles away. She smiled contently as she shared the meal with her sister friends.

DANCE OF LOVE

Respectfully and lovingly, we held hands from a distant, straight out like in high school, my right hand in his left with a two feet clearance between us as we internalized the music...still...not moving yet inwardly moving as we heard the beat...the rhythm...listening to the music and flowing with the flow...waiting for the appropriate time to move in unison. Gently, I was led across and around the floor, floating, swaying, sailing, escalating...in rhythm together like Ginger Rogers and Fred Astaire. We looked to opposite directions as we danced: he to the left and me to the right. Occasionally, our eyes met and smiled as we enjoyed the dance of love.

MOVE UP A LITTLE HIGHER

Shoes, I couldn't see his shoes. That bothered me. It's important to see the shoes, I've been told. You can tell a lot about a man by the shoes he wears. What type of shoes might they be? Black and shiny? Tennis shoes? Open toed like sandals? Loafers? Stacey Adams? Spectators or some other expensive shoe? The first few seconds, I tried to see his shoes but couldn't help but move up a little higher.

He wore white freshly pressed Bermuda shorts, with a fullness in the front center, slightly to the left. His shorts wonderfully contracted with the smooth skin color of his exercised legs. "Hummm! Whooo! Help me!"

I moved up a little higher and saw a white caftan shirt with v-neck collar that exposed his long, kissable, beautiful neck. His firm arms begged to be displayed under his three quarter length shirt sleeves.

I moved up a little higher. A white scarf was pulled back in a large knot to the back of his head. "How exotic!" I thought.

My unknown lover wore a beautiful smile wide with sparkling white teeth. It was a warm, sincere smile, from a distant, for me, I hoped, but it could have been for anyone who noticed.

WOMAN IN BLUE

Mid-block, in front of parked cars, stood a woman in blue. Thumb gingerly hiked for a pickup, she mouthed, "How about a ride? Come on," as she maintained eye contact with each man in a passing car.

"Okay, pretty please," she continued as she put her hands together in prayer. Men stared at her as they slowly moved along with traffic.

Another car was approaching. The woman in blue sighed and looked up to the sky as she pulled her tank top down from the bottom to expose all but her nipples, leaned forward and then up with a smile as she licked her lips. Immediately, she commanded attention, got her ride and so did the men that followed.

SUGAR TIT

Suck it when it's big and sweet.
Suck it when it's a little tit.
Suck it until it's dry.
Now, who do you think is gonna die?
You baby son of a bitch.

HONEY, BABY, SUGAR, DEAR

My family and very close friends can call me by my nickname or other words of endearment.   Nick names and such are not allowed to be used by strangers, peers, superiors and other business relationships.

If my boyfriend calls me Honey, Baby, Sugar or Dear, he will quickly be told to scream out my name-- not Honey, Baby, Sugar or Dear.   I want him to know that he is with me. That's the way it was until I met one who called me Doll so beau-ti-ful-ly.

SOMETHING LIGHT

Babe, I want to be intimate with you. You know a man has needs. When I don't, things start to hurt. Babe, I want to be with you, TONIGHT.

I should have known something was wrong when he didn't call me by my name. "Babe!" Do you want a safe receptacle or me? Where's love? I desire, want and am looking for accountability and commitment. Is that you? Are you the one?

Well, why not. It will help me pass the night, something light.

SUPERFICIAL

I don't know you. You don't know me, nor do you seem to want to. I do you but you don't want to know anything about me, too seriously. Yet, you say you're serious about me. I seriously want to know you before, I get seriously involved with you.

THE LIGHT

It's been said that it is the darkest before light. Well, I was in the dark. I've finally figured it out. We were on different wave lengths. To him, intimate meant sex. To me, it meant sharing one's thoughts, problems, joys, goals etc.

To you, I was a novelty affair. I still want a relationship. Now, I know why I slowly dropped you. Finally, I see the night in something light. Before daylight, I'll set my life right.

"Sunshine With Some Drizzle"
  Dr. Charleszetta Stalling

SWEET HEART

When I talk with him or hear him call me and say, "Hi Sweetheart," I feel a softness come over me and I'm mellow. He embraces me with his love and I willingly welcome it. I'm joyful, with a wide, silly looking grin on my face from ear to ear. I know because I looked in the mirror to see why the corners of my mouth were hurting. I am content. I let go and enjoy the minutes, sometimes 90 minutes or more of talking on the phone. I am having a loving long distant relationship with a gentleman.

Baby, you excite me! Just thinking of you is a turn on. I feel like I think a teenager might feel in love, although, I was never in love as a teenager. I feel more for him than my ex-husband of 17 years. Now, I reflect upon my past and why I married. I cared for my ex, let him convince me while at the same time I reasoned it was about time to marry and have a family. Maybe, this is not a fair comparison since I have been divorced since 1988. Wow!! That was 17 years ago. That's the same number of years I was married. Then again, maybe, time changes feelings as well perceptions.

With my new friend, I get off on the smallest of gestures. When he first gave me a firm yet gentle hug, it was a good thing he couldn't see my face. I inhaled, and exhaled as I rolled my eyes upward toward the starry blue sky. What a stimulating sensation. "Oh, my, my, my," I mouthed to myself. New relationships are exciting!!!! I want to shout.

BECAUSE JUST BETTY JEAN

Because just you BJ can do what you do. I was thinking of you and praying the best for you.

When I saw this cloth of art, I knew it was you and something you would like.   It was bold.   It was colorful.

It radiated life of beautiful people of color dancing and singing: Day-Oh, Matilda, Chi-Chi Bud Oh, and Yellow Bird.

The cloth shared love: Water Came to My Eyes, Love Alone and of course, Big Bamboo.

Because you live life, share love, give and strive to walk in the light of righteousness, I dedicate this to you on your special day and that's every day.

Because just, there is no other uniquely like you, BJ.

"Sunshine With Some Drizzle"
Dr. Charleszetta Stalling

II. JACKSON STORIES STRECHED

DANCING A JIG

My papa rented land from old man Jones. Although, he had his own land, Papa share cropped with Mr. Jones.

Our father didn't like for us kids to work in the hot sun. So at the crack of dawn, we started picking fruit and vegetables. Mr. Jones would sometimes bring a chair to the field to sit and watch us work.

When my brother Dave and I took a break, we would dance and dance. As we danced, we moved closer and closer to old man Jones. Usually, we danced so hard and wild, we couldn't help it if we bumped into his chair and knocked him down to the ground. We accidently did this to the old man at least two or three times.

Old man Jones got tired of our mess. He complained to Papa about what his kids did to him. He told and showed Papa simultaneously how we twisted our hips, pointed our fingers in the air while shaking our heads and dancing a jig.

Papa slowly moved his head from right to left in disbelief, and thought that old man Jones must finally be going crazy from sitting too long in the sun.

"Where did my kids get the music to dance to?" Papa asked.

"There weren't none," replied old man Jones.

Right then and there Papa knew for sure that old man Jones was not going crazy. He was crazy. Papa knew that people could not dance a jig without music.

IT'S IN THE BLOOD

Papa's prayers shook the entire house. From my bedroom, I knew he was praying but I couldn't clearly understand them. So, I used to get up to hear my Papa's prayers, then I knew what was on his mind. He talked to God like he was in the same room. When Papa prayed, he didn't stutter, his prayers made my hair stand up; I could feel the prayers in my whole body.

If somebody mistreated Papa or anybody in his family, he would call them by name, and say what he did to remedy the situation--after he said what he wanted. He ended all of his prayers by asking for God's guidance and help according to HIS will. People didn't want Papa to put his mouth on them.

Papa was really concerned about my brother and me dancing. Eventually, my brother, Dave stopped dancing. I continued to dance until I heard my father praying for me one night in the dining room.

"Lord, Lord, please hear my prayer." I couldn't help but hear it roar in the quiet of midnight. "My child, Ruth, dances everywhere she goes. Please wet her parched lips if she goes below. Thank you, Lord."

I didn't dance anymore after that prayer. I didn't want to go to hot hell. Once I was grown, I mentioned the incident to my father. He chuckled, "It worked, didn't it?"

"Yes, I still like to dance, but I don't. My daughter, Charlie does."

I'LL DO IT

"Freddie go to the country store to get five pounds of sugar for the family. Don't tarry. Go straight there and straight back. You hear?" asked but really said by Papa.

"Yes, Papa," Freddie said as an obedient child.

Freddie was on his way when he got distracted by a frog. He got down on all fours and hopped like the frog. Up, down, up, down, he jumped.

Then he saw a rooster run after a chicken. So he ran after the rooster that chased the chicken. He flapped his arms and squealed, "Squawk, squawk."

As he ran, he came across a puddle of water collected from the rain. There it was directly in his path. Freddie couldn't resist jumping across it. He jumped back and forth over it several times.

By now, Freddie was ready for a snack. In front of him was a peach tree with one large peach within his reach. He ate it as juice ran down his cheek.

Freddie felt so good. He smiled, rubbed his stomach and patted his head at the same time.

Papa looked out the window at Freddie. His dark brown eyes saw everything Freddie did. After a while he called out to Freddie, "That's Okay, I'll do it. Come on in."

"Yes, Papa," said Freddie.   He was glad he didn't have to go to the store.

The screen door opened and Freddie was snatched in like a whirl wind by Papa and given a spanking.

Freddie learned as we all did.   Hop to do it when told by Papa or Mama.   Watch out for "I will do it."   If chores were not done, they would do it to you.   That is, give you a spanking, and you would still have to do whatever it was anyway.

EYE IN THE CORNER

Sometimes Mother goes on various errands. Before leaving, she gives us work assignments to complete while she is gone. She wants to keep us busy so that we don't get into any mischief.

"I'm going to leave my eye in the corner." We nervously looked around at the corners to see which corner Mother might leave her eye, but she looked at each of us. "I'll be back as soon as I can. Be good."

As soon as Mother left, we stuffed a rag in each corner of the room, that way she couldn't see what we were doing in her absence. We danced. We stuck our fingers in the jelly, killed and fried the biggest chicken. Accidently, we broke Mother's big brown jug that she kept on the fire place mantle. We sweep up the pieces from the jug and made sure the house was clean. After we finished doing what we wanted to do, we removed the rags from the corners.

When Mother got home, she looked at each of us. "My eye has seen some goings on. Speak now." She got out the broom. "This broom knows," said Mother in a slow deep low voice. Mother suspiciously looked around, with wide accusing eyes, at the young ones around her.

"Broom, help my eye to find the young one(s) who killed my big chicken I was saving for Sunday. Let me know who broke my big brown jug that sat on the mantle?" It was then that we realized that Mother had left her eye in the broom and not in a corner.

"Sunshine With Some Drizzle"
   Dr. Charleszetta Stalling

We stared at each other. The whites of our eyes nervously blinked back—silently. No lips moved. We stood frozen still.

"This broom," said Mother as she held it menacingly with two hands over her right shoulder, "is going to knock the brains out of the child who did it unless he or she confesses. Line up one at a time and walk under the broom as I hold it above you."

Mother held the broom just above our heads. "Broom, as each one walks under your arm, examine him, see if he's telling the truth. If so, let him pass. If not, beat the devil out and put some sense into him so that I won't have to kill him." More often than not, one or more of us confessed.

It paid to tell the truth. That was a mighty big broom and could probably knock some brains out in addition to killing one's back.

FIRE-A-WAY

There had not been a good crop for a couple of years. Bills were piling up. Daily needs and expenses for twelve plus children continued. There were whispers of sending us to stay with various relatives.

Even though the farm was practically paid for, vultures started moving in for the final kill. They wanted to purchase the farm for far less than its value. They knew the value of the house alone was worth twice the offer presented. There was land too, but they wanted the house. Pressure was put on. The pressure was so strong and hot it created a fire.

Luckily, we all got out without damage. The house fired away and burned to the ground. Everything in it was burned.

Some of us children slept in the big wagons. Others moved to the barn to have a roof over their heads. A few were glad to sleep under the stars.

Mysteriously, our blankets, pillows and clothing reappeared. When we got hungry, we found canned fruit, vegetables and butter along the back wall of the barn. Under hay stacks we discovered big sacks of flour, sugar and cornmeal.

The pictures we had in the house appeared on the barn walls. It almost felt like home. We kept the barn neat and clean--cleaner than I keep my house now.

The smoke house wasn't burned so we searched to see what we could find. In it were cast iron skillets and pots. We discovered that we had all the meat we needed in the smoke house, pork, ham and bacon. We used the smoke house as a kitchen, we cooked and ate there.

The folks were no longer interested in the land, for the house had fired away. Slowly, the house was rebuilt and we moved back in. We had a good crop the next year and for many more years.

FREE SHOTS

Free shots were being offered in town for those who qualified. Grandpa heard about the wonders of the free shots: one neighbor told grandpa how the shot really helped his back; another how it helped his rheumatism; and another the arthritics in his knees.

Grandpa decided he would go and get one of those free shots. He had a bad back, too. After an examination, it was determined that he didn't need one.

"Tuss my socks." That was grandpa's way of cursing, for he never did in his entire life. "Those infernal folks refused to give me a free shot."

Grandpa didn't know that the shots were for various sexual diseases. And the men about town were not about to tell him or anybody the real purpose of the shot.

TAKE BACK YOUR MONEY

Grandpa and Grandma had a saving in the local bank for many years. It wasn't easy, but they managed to squeeze away some money for really hard times.

One day, the banker came to our home to talk with Grandpa. He wondered what the banker wanted. Grandpa invited him in, told him to have a seat and directed one of us kids to fetch him cool fresh water from the well.

The banker seemed nice. He held his hat in his hand, called Grandpa, Mr. Jackson. Grandpa and the banker greeted each other. They chit chatted about the weather and the current crops.

The banker seemed nervous. He looked down at his hat and moved it about. Finally, he advised Grandpa to take his money out the bank as soon as possible.

The banker stood up. Grandpa stood up, too and said, "Thank you for coming by."

"Have a good day, Mr. Jackson. I wish you and your family well," he said with a slight bow of his head as he left our home.

Grandpa listened to him. After the banker left, Papa said, "He don't want our money no more."

From another room, Grandma listened to what the banker said, too. The next day, bright and early, Grandma got dressed and went to town. She went to the bank and checked out all their money.

A day later, the bank went bankrupt. Many well to do folks lost lots of money, but we didn't. We took back all of our money.

AN AFFAIR WITH A CHICKEN

Ernest worked hard driving his 18 wheel truck across country. When at home on the weekends, he manicured the lawn, cleaned his cars until they glowed and gambled with his buddies in our garage.

Usually, Ernest only gambled a small amount of money. Things were fine with my mother and stepfather until he lost ALL of his week's earnings gambling.

When my step-father didn't give my Mother money to buy groceries, she didn't say anything about it. She was sweet as pecan pie. She gave him a kiss on the cheek and told him to get ready for dinner.

On that Sunday, baked chicken was served with cabbage, peas and carrots, steamed rice and corn bread.

For breakfast, on Monday morning, Mother served chicken croquets. She made him a chicken sandwich on wheat for lunch. A large chicken pot-pie with carrots and peas was served for dinner.

On Tuesday morning, Mother served scrambled eggs and diced chicken for breakfast. For lunch, Ernest had chicken salad with lots of raw onions and celery that he did not like. There was still plenty of chicken pot pie left from Monday, so they ate the rest for dinner.

Tuesday night, Mother soaked and cooked a large pot of pinto beans. On Wednesday, we had beans with shredded chicken for breakfast, lunch and dinner.

By mid-week, Ernest was not looking forward to breakfast, lunch or dinner. But, he didn't say anything about the meals. Neither did Mother.

My brother and I dare say nothing, but we suffered, too. At least, we had a break when we ate school lunches.

Mother thought about how she could creatively create additional chicken dishes for the rest of the week.

By Thursday morning, Ernest didn't want any food prepared by Mother. For breakfast, he crumbled left over cold cornbread, added to it one raw beaten egg and buttermilk and then gulped it down. He forgot his lunch. Mother smiled to herself.

There was hardly any chicken left. Mother boiled the chicken bones and scrapes and made chicken soup. It certainly did smell good with the fresh herbs from the garden.

Mother could hardly wait to serve the dinner. She set the table with good china, linen napkins, silver eating utensils and lit red candles. Ernest and my Mother sat down at the table. The blessing was said. "A real meal at last," thought Ernest. He opened the top of the soup bowl and saw a watery broth with scrapes of chicken and skin. He couldn't take it anymore. "If you give me anymore chicken, I'm going to cluck like a chicken!"

Mother smiled. "I'll be glad to fix any meal you want when you give me money for food." Ernest brought his hard earned money home every week after his affair with chicken.

RAW DEAL

While my cousin, Prentice, was in the service, the base had a big dinner, all the food you could possibly imagine. The men ate and drank from the main table.

On a small table, there was a beautifully browned pig with a red apple in its mouth. The men were instructed not to touch it.

Prentice and the other men continued to eat and drink, but they kept looking at the beautifully browned pig with the red apple in its mouth.

The challenge was on. When the officers were not looking, Prentice and some of the men stole the beautifully browned pig with the red apple in its mouth. They buried it in the snow.

Meanwhile, each of the men involved with hiding the pig took eating utensils, condiments and bread for a late snack. On the way to their barracks they dug up the beautifully browned pig with the apple in its mouth.

Yes, they were ready for a midnight snack. "Ready for a check?" asked my cousin Prentice. In anticipation for the food, they licked their lips as they prepared to respond.

"Bread?" asked Prentice.

"Here!"

"Forks?"

"Here!"

"Mayo?"

"Here!"

"Mustard?" continued Prentice.

"Here!"

"Knife?"

"Here!"

Prentice picked up the knife and cut the pig. Blood squirted everywhere. The pig was raw but beautifully browned with a red apple in its mouth.

III.   UGANDAN GLIMPSES

PEACE

Lie on the green grass to cool
Tarmac road to warm
Walk under the rain for calm

"Sunshine With Some Drizzle"
Dr. Charleszetta Stalling

GLIMPSES FROM THE BUS

Children wave with glee
Goats squat to pee
Wild boas kneel to eat
Malibu Storks we eye and let be

PLAYING CHICKEN

Hen sits on side of the road
Hen stands in the road
Happy hen plays on the road
Squash! Flat hen on road
Fat chicken cooks in the pot
Yumm, chicken tonight

LOVE YOU TO DEATH

Otis, the elevator, was lonely.
Three people came within.
He clasped his jaws tight.
Stubbornly, he refused to move.

Scared people were engulfed.
No air, light, phone or bell.
"I'll keep them incubated and warm,"
Otis thought. "Maybe, I'll love them to death."

Reluctantly, he was forced to release his grasp.
Out jumped his children, elated to be free.
Once again, Otis was left alone,
Lonely with an empty nest.

DIGNIFIED MOTHER

She knows not her beauty
Balanced basket on her crown
Eloquently dressed
With thong dusty feet
Her royalty radiates as
She struts to make thin ends meet

WALKING BIKES

Heavy green banana stalks
Go home or market
Straddled on worn walking bikes

CONTRADICTORY BEHAVIOR

They don't barter here.
He emphatically shook his head, no.
They don't barter here.
Look around, he has nice things.
I brought all these folks!
How much for my shirt?   he asked the owner.
He got a discount, but not the other folks.
For there's no bartering here.

"Sunshine With Some Drizzle"
Dr. Charleszetta Stalling

SOME MAN

In America, unsure
But, in Africa
He swaggers with chest way out

AUGUST 2nd
TORORO/BOSUMBATYA, UGANDA

Four girls in green leaf dresses

Parade through the town

"How, cute," we say 'til we learn

It's circumcision day.

IV. GROWING UP/ CHILDHOOD EXPERIENCES

THE BIG, BULKY, BURGUNDY JACKET

Flop! Something large and soft fell on Freddie's feet in the crowded small closet.   Startled, Freddie looked down.   "Ugh!   It's that big, bulky, burgundy jacket," said Freddie.   "It's uglier than I remembered."

"I hid this jacket in my closet a year ago.   Mother must have forgotten about it, also.   I bet this jacket is too small, now.   Hee, hee," Freddie giggled.   "I've grown four inches taller this year.   My arms are longer.   My chest is larger and my shoulders are broader. I'm bigger all over!"

"Sunshine With Some Drizzle"
    Dr. Charleszetta Stalling

~ 32 ~

"I will put on the jacket to show Mother that it is too small." Freddie hated the jacket but his Mother loved it. "What? That's strange!" said Freddie. "This big, bulky, burgundy jacket fits me perfectly." He wiggled his shoulders comfortably in the jacket. It was snugly and warm. He felt safe and protected. Freddie looked at himself in the mirror. "I look handsome in this big, bulky, burgundy jacket." His mother agreed.

"I like this big, bulky burgundy jacket," said Freddie. He liked the jacket so much that he took care of it. He spent time with it. He wore it every day of the week...Monday, Tuesday, Wednesday, Thursday and Friday. Freddie even wore the jacket on Saturday and Sunday.

When Freddie didn't wear the big, bulky, burgundy jacket, he cuddled it under his arm. He cleaned it and hung it up neatly, on a hanger in the closet. At night, he used the jacket as a pillow.

The big, bulky, burgundy jacket kept Freddie warm in the winter. It was most unusual--it kept him cool in the summer and dry in the rain without getting wet–and it was not a rain coat.

Gradually, Freddie began to really enjoy and like his jacket. "No," he thought, "I love my big, bulky, burgundy jacket." The jacket listened and curled up under his warm hugs. It felt safe and protected.

One day the jacket thought and said "I love you too, Freddie, although you may not know. I will grow as you grow. Then we will always be together. I will not wear out because you care for me." The big, bulky, burgundy jacket gave Freddie a warm, long hug.

Freddie wore the jacket all through elementary school. He wore it in the first, second, third, fourth, fifth and sixth grade. Freddie grew and grew and so did the big, bulky, burgundy jacket.

Freddie wore the jacket in junior high school through the seventh, eighth and ninth grade. Freddie grew and grew and so did the big, bulky, burgundy jacket.

In high school, Freddie went to the tenth, eleventh and the twelfth grade. Freddie grew and grew and so did the big, bulky, burgundy jacket.

When Freddie graduated from college guess what he wore under his graduation robe? Yes, the big, bulky, burgundy jacket.

Freddie and his jacket had many good years growing together. The jacket was proud of Freddie because he stayed in school. It almost burst at its seams with happiness. The jacket helped Freddie in a big way. It kept him warm in the winter and cool in the summer and very happy. That's the end of the story about the big, bulky, burgundy jacket.

BED WETTING

When my brother, Baba, wet the bed, he would do one of two things: stay in bed as long as he could; or hide behind the hill, near the house, in his wet pajamas.

Everyone knew he hid behind the same hill each time. He would stay there until someone loudly announced, "Breakfast is ready."

Slowly, he would raise his head and his large dark brown eyes over the hill. From the kitchen, we could see him lift his nose to the air and lick his lips.

Baba's stomach started to growl, "Wonder what good things there are to eat? Is that smell bacon or sausage? Muffins or pancakes? Wonder if that smell is fried potatoes with onions?"

Eventually, he was compelled by the smells to withdraw from his secret hiding place. He knew there were two things, no three things in store for him: a bawling out; dry clothes; and a delicious breakfast. Well, tomorrow was another day to try to stay dry.

PATTY CAKE

As the two older brothers, age three and six played with their Power Rangers, I entertained the youngest. Singing and playing patty cake with my one year old grandson sitting on my lap, I said, "Patty cake, patty cake, baker's man. Make me a cake as fast as you can."

"No, no," interjected my three year old grandson. "That's wrong! It's patty cake, patty cake, baker's man. You make me mad."

Lightly, I tried to convince him. He was not moved to change his opinion. He was set with his righteousness and looked at me like I was the mistaken one.

"Here comes Power Ranger, again," said the oldest brother. Our conversation was lost as soon as it started. "Zoom," said the three year old brother in response.

THE TV DINNER

"Mom, can we get a TV dinner?" my son asked as we were riding home one day from school.

"Why do you want a TV dinner?" This is incredible I thought to myself. Why would anyone want a TV dinner over a home cooked meal? I take pride in preparing meals from scratch, no short cuts for me. Even when my son was a baby, I prepared fresh food for him. I didn't purchased those little off colored jars of baby food that looked like vomit.

"Kids at school say they are really, really good. Their Moms' fix them all the time. Please, can we get one?"

"Sure! What kind do you want?"

"I don't know?"

"Let's go to the store, now. You can pick out one of the meals for kids."

My son looked at the different choices. Finally he decided on the little hotdogs and baked bean dinner.

While the oven heated, we read the directions for preparation. "Bake at 350 degrees for 20 minutes without removing tin foil cover."

Finally the TV dinner was ready. He was excited about tasting the 'really good' TV dinner.

"Doesn't that smell good," he said. We opened it. There appeared to be only one small hotdog. My son leaned closer as he stirred the beans looking for more hotdogs. He couldn't find any more.

"This is not like the picture on the outside of the box. That one has lots of little hotdogs." He decided to taste the beans anyway. "These are so-so," he said, "I'm mad!"

"What do you want to do about it?"

"Let's write to tell them about the one little hotdog."

"What do you want to say?" My son talked aloud. He said what he wanted to say then wrote the letter with some assistance from me.

Three weeks later, we received an apology letter from the company with coupons for two TV dinners. We selected two free TV dinners, one for him and one for me.

After eating his TV dinner unenthusiastically, my son said, "Mom, I think I like your food better."

"Yes!" Tell the world, I exclaimed to myself. "Thank you, son," calmly I smiled, "I appreciate your compliment."

SPEECH TRAINING NEEDED

"Today at school, we had a speaker from a southern university to share Black History. He seemed really knowledgeable but he said it in a boring way. He didn't know how to speak. Students clapped before he finished his last few words. We wanted to get rid of him. I thought about referring him to you," shared my son.

"What a compliment! He really does listen to what and how I say things. Public speaking with Toast Masters, International, is paying off," I thought.

MAGIC FISH

"Mama Lu, Mama Lu.   There are fish in your back yard!"

"Fish?"

"Yes, Mama Lu."

"What are they doing?" asked Mama Lu.

"Just splashing around in the mud," said Jackie

"Humm."

"They're just flopping around.   How did they get there, Mama Lu?"

"From the rain and the sun."

"The rain and the sun?"

"Yes," she repeated with a confirming nod of her gray head.

"The sun soaked them up from the river and the rain rained them down."

Curious, Mama Lu asked, "What do the fish look like?"

"Oh, they are about this long," exclaimed Jackie as she extended her hands about four inches apart. "They are the most beautiful colors."

Grandma started to think back to her childhood. She remembered seeing fish of a similar description.

Curious, Grandma asked, "What are their colors?"

"Oh! They are red, orange, blue, green and gold." Jackie jumped about like the fish as she described them. Suddenly, she stopped, stood with her forefinger on her chin, thinking. "They look like rainbows, rainbows splashing all around."

"Yes, like rainbows," Grandma nodded her head up and down, getting more excited by the minute. She remembered seeing such fish as a child numerous times. She smiled reminiscently looking up at her granddaughter as she jumped about in glee.

"Grandma, they make the most wonderful music without singing."

"Yes, child, yes, heavenly music."

"Yes, heavenly music." Jackie was so pleased that her Grandmother seemed to truly understand and experience what she was experiencing. She wondered, "How did you know it was heavenly music?"

"I know because you described magic fish."

"How do you know that they are magic fish?   Will they grant three wishes or something?"

"Humm, maybe, maybe not."

"Maybe, maybe not.   What does that mean, Grandma Lu?"
"Sometimes, the magic fish did grant my wishes many, many years ago.   Sometimes, they didn't.   The magic fish didn't count too well.   That is, if I was only to get three wishes.   I didn't count either.   I was too glad to get them.   Maybe, they did it on purpose."

"Are there really magic fish?"

"Maybe, maybe not."

"I wonder if they will grant my wishes?" asked Jackie. "Thanks Grandma Lu."   Jackie ran outside, to the backyard, to talk with the beautiful rainbow colored magic fish that made heavenly music without singing.

HAIR WINGS

Tomorrow is picture day, I am so excited. Mother washed and dried my hair last night. Early the next morning, Mother pressed and curled my hair. Mother gave me a curled pony tail and wide bangs. I looked pretty.

The peak of the school day was taking our individual and class pictures. Finally, it came, the teacher told the entire class, "Go to the rest room, put a little water on your hair and make it pretty."

My best friend, Marion, the other girls and I ran to the rest room to do as our teacher instructed us. We put water on our hair to enhance our individual styles. As we gazed in the mirror, one of my classmates asked me, "Are you suppose to do that?"

"Sure, the teacher told us to." The same girl shrugged her shoulders and continued to wet her hair as Marion and I did.

When I got home that afternoon, Mother asked me, "Where did you get those wings?"

"What wings?"

"The ones above your ears!" I ran to look in the mirror. I felt my hair. It stood out on both sides above my ears. They indeed did appear as wings that refused to close.

"Sunshine With Some Drizzle"
  Dr. Charleszetta Stalling

"What happened?" Mother asked. I told her.

Mother managed to restrain herself until she saw my pictures two weeks later. There I was with a big snag-a-toothed grin and hair wings above my ears. Mother was really upset with the teacher for not being sensitive to hair differences and possibly other differences. Also, she was upset with herself for not explaining our unique and versatile hair to me. On top of that, she was studying to become a beautician.

Me, I didn't know any better. Nor did I realize that there were only two of us Black girls in the class. My best girlfriend, Marion, had wash and wear hair that she could put water on. My hair was quite different. My hair napped up, if it looked like rain. Now, I know that nappy hair or any hair is good hair.

V. GROWING PAINS—REFLECTIONS

PAIN IS PAIN

She stood in the middle of the road.   Her blank face showed nothing, her eyes nor mouth moved, her eyes told it all. Sadly, she stared down at the mangled disfigured bloody body.

Seeing this, I slowed my car to give her time to move.   With silent quietness, as in respect, my car slowly approached.

Without looking, sensing my coming, she moved decidedly out of the way.   She spread her wings and flew to the sidelines to look again.

I felt sadness for the black bird's pain.   Perhaps, I should stop and pick up the dead bird.   Then what would I do with it? Give it to the other bird?   Bury it or what?   Have a funeral? I'm ashamed to say, I drove on.

"Sunshine With Some Drizzle"
   Dr. Charleszetta Stalling

HE-MAN WITH PACIFIER

With a pacifier in his mouth, stood a man watching and waiting for the signal to change so that he could cross the street.

He had a one-year old baby balanced on his right shoulder while he held both feet with one hand. On the left shoulder, he had a diaper bag and held the hand of a girl child of three.

He looked right, left and behind before he crossed the street. As he walked across, the baby felt free to flap her arms as though she was flying up and down.

The lady in the car in front of me, leaned out her window, lightly honked her horn, said something complimentary as she laughed, smiled and nodded her head in confirmation of what she saw.

The He-man with pacifier in his mouth, glanced her way, nodded his head in thanks and continued up the way.

111° IN THE SUN

A slight brush of air was created as he peddled his bike forward toward the humid hot air.   He pushed his head out front of his body to catch it.   His face bore no expression.

On his soiled worn brown rimed hat he donned a feather above each ear with a fresh light pink flower in the middle. His long sleeve green and black plaid shirt protected him from sunburn but not the heat.

He stood on his bike to pump harder as sweat ran down his shinny stained blue denim jeans.   Get out of the way he seemed to say as he possessively sped his bike in the car lanes.

COLORED GREENS

End of January, or early February is the best time to pick wild mustard greens. My mother and I planned to pick greens–rain or shine. When my sister friend, Thelma, called, I asked if she wanted to come, too. She said, "Great! I have always wanted to, but I don't know how or what to pick." I told her that my Mother would explain everything and to wear a rain coat just in case it rained.

We picked up my sister friend, Thelma and searched for an exclusive area to pick greens. We found an ideal vacant grassy area between two half-million dollar homes. The rain started just as we opened the car doors to get out.

Mother put on her bright red rain coat, Thelma her yellow raincoat, and I my purple raincoat. We were a happy sight in our colored coats laughing, bending, picking and stuffing wild mustards and turnips greens in our plastic shopping bags while it continued to rain.

My mother shared how to recognize wild mustard. "Look for yellow flowers or small clusters like broccoli at top of plant." Mother and I could tell that they were tender because we would break the leaves from the stems with ease without pulling the plant up.

An older Black man looked at us women picking greens and said, "Let me know when they are ready and I'll come help you eat them." We laughed, "We will yell for you to come when they are ready. Then again, we might play like Little Red Hen."

A little while later, a young man with dreg locks stopped his car, leaned his head out the passenger window and asked, "Are all of those greens?"

"Many are. There's a lot of tall grass, too. Come and join us. We have some extra bags. My Mother will show you what to pick." He gladly got out of his car and joined us.

A young lady jogging, jogged in place, up and down, "Hi, are you picking greens?"

"Yes. There are plenty here."

"I need to hurry home to tell my grandmother about the greens. We'll be back. Thanks!" She said as she jogged away, smiling.

Other people passed us riding in their cars. Many honked and waved cheerfully. A few growled and turned their heads away from us after looking to see what we were doing in THEIR neighborhood.

After picking greens for a while, my Mother exclaimed, "Honey, my back is hurting!" She straightened up with both hands on her hips and took a deep breath.

We stopped picking greens and looked toward my mother. As we did, we saw a beautiful rainbow caressing her and ... all of us. We had fun picking colored greens that day.

A week later, I passed the wild mustard green lot and noted that the greens had been plowed under. The green greens were not a fire hazard. It wasn't summertime nor was it hot. I wonder why they cut down the colored greens ?

"Sunshine With Some Drizzle"
   Dr. Charleszetta Stalling

MUCH TO DO

So much to do.   But I do not
I write what is in my heart... now
I cry, for I need a cleansing and purification
To reach a clarification of death and
How to peacefully and joyfully accept.

CRYING GOOD TIME

The beauty God creates is magnificent and awesome. His
creation really registered, today; the freshness of the green
irregular shaped trees against the clear blue sky brought tears
of joy that rolled down my face to the side of my nose and into
my mouth. Yes, salty tears. I had a crying good time
praising God, the Father and His son Jesus Christ.

FLOWERS

Today, I was going to buy flowers when
I saw all of the beautiful ones in my own yard.
I was only gone two days.
When did they appear?
Did they just bloom?
Or did I just notice?

LEARNING TO WAIT

What a beautiful picture! Wish I had a camera to capture it. She sat on the sidewalk with her long legs fully extended and crossed at the ankles. Alone, a Black girl, approximately 15 to 18 years of age, sat with her back against the red stained fence as she held open a book. She seemed to be totally submerged in her reading while she waited patiently for the public bus. Her braids cascaded on both sides of her face as she released a slow smile in response to what she was reading or perhaps thinking. I smiled too.

"Sunshine With Some Drizzle"
Dr. Charleszetta Stalling

TRUE KINDNESS AND LOVE

Sleep! Sleep, I told myself. I hadn't slept for several days. Some grayish-black cat that was still a young kitten decided to have kittens in my one-store house--the attic of all places. I noticed her jumping from the outside ledge of my dining room window up under the eve of the crisscrossing 90 degree angle roof. I thought, well, that's okay. I thought so until... I began to hear strange unusual sounds emanating from the ceiling of my bathroom.

"Do you hear that?" I asked my son.

"No," he said as he looked at me with raised eyebrows.

"I have good hearing, and I hear some things moving up there... in the ceiling," I stated empathically. This went on for several days.

Whenever I heard noises from above, I ran to get someone to confirm my hearing. My boyfriend heard nothing. My son heard nothing. One time, I gathered both of them in my small bathroom to listen to the sounds I just heard. "Listen," I said. They heard nothing. They both looked at each other and then at me like I was hearing things or going crazy. I didn't hear anything this minute either.

The noises usually started about 4:30 AM and continued for 30 to 40 minutes.   Eventually, I would fall asleep.

"Meow, meow."

"Oh no," I exclaimed.   "Kittens!"

Finally, my son and boyfriend heard what I heard. "Hallelujah, I'm not crazy or hearing things."

I hadn't rested well for about one week.   It was time for that cat and her kittens to get out of my house.   This was an invasion.   I didn't care that the cat lived in my house before I bought it.   It was not my problem that the previous owner left his cats over a year ago.

When I saw the dull black colored mother kitten crossing my roof, looking thin, tired, timid, and apprehensive, I said aloud, "Okay you can stay a little longer, but as soon as you are able--please move.   I need some rest.   At least be quiet."

Quiet she was.   No longer did she awaken me at 4:30 A.M. Things were well between us until my son heard kitten sounds somewhere in the roof of his bathroom.

"Meow, meow, meow!"

"The mother cat will get the kittens," I assured my son.

"Sunshine With Some Drizzle"
  Dr. Charleszetta Stalling

After two days, the meows got weaker. My son crawled into the attic. Eventually he found the meowing kittens. Two of them were trapped in a metal tubing about 18 inches deep. He tried to reach them, but he couldn't.

I went to a neighbor's house that I had met several days earlier and explained the situation. The wife said, "My husband will come to help you in fifteen minutes."

My neighbor came in overalls, prepared to crawl in the attic. My son led the way. Together, they were able to rescue the kittens in my son's bathroom. We put them in a basket.

"Now, I will be able to get some peace," I said aloud.

"Meow, meow!" There were more sounds coming from the other side of the house, in my bathroom, not from the ceiling but under the floor. My neighbor crawled under the house and pin pointed the location. With my permission, he cut a hole in the floor and pulled out two more kittens. We added the them to the other kittens for a total of four.

My son looked at the four kittens and asked, "Can I keep one?"

Reluctantly, I said, "Yes." He selected the smallest one. Picked it up and softly caressed it near his chest. It looked like a weakling to me.

"Thank you, Mom."

"You are most welcome, son. Now the caring of your cat begins."

I thanked my neighbor and insisted that he take some money for his assistance. He shared that both he and his wife did animal rescue. Further that they worked with veterinarians and could get the cats neutered or spayed and could obtain homes for them.

"Great!" I was so pleased that the kittens would get their shots and placed in loving homes. My neighbor across from me accepted one cat. Now, we only had to find placement for the other two cats.

My son named his cat Magic, after the basketball player, because his mother could jump from the window ledge to under the roof.

Several months later, after Magic became stronger, we noted that she took after her mother — she could really jump, too.

RAINY DAY

Why? Why did it have to rain on me, today?
It's raining, now.   Perhaps, I can walk later.
Mother's getting older.   I knew she was but didn't really.
I don't like nor want to accept it, but I am forced to.
It's life.   If we live, we do grow older.
I do love her...unconditionally.

DON'T LEAVE HOME WITHOUT IT

As I walked to the kitchen to get my cup of lukewarm coffee, I noticed that my sixteen year old son had left his textbook on the kitchen counter. While still in my robe and house shoes, I grabbed my car keys and the book to meet my son at the bus stop before the public bus arrived.

As I was driving up the street, he was running back toward our home. I caught his eyes and held up his book. I got you covered son, I thought. He emphatically shook his head no and kept running up the street. He did not get in the car. I turned around the car and headed home. He beat me there, unlocked the front door and ran inside.

I decided to wait for him in the driveway with the engine running. Less than one minute later, he ran out the house and jumped in the car and looked straight ahead. He did not say anything. I proceeded to drive him toward the bus stop. My curiosity got the best of me, I had to ask, "What did you do or get?"

"My deodorant," he said.

VI. ALMOST GROWN/ MATURING REFLECTIONS

STILL THE SAME

"Can you tell that I have lost weight?"

"No, Mom. I can't tell when you gain or when you lose. You look the same to me as you did when I was six years old."

Flattered and pleased, I grinned widely. "Oh, wait a minute. What about last week when you starred at the gray hair in the middle of my head as I blow dried it."

"Well, you do look the same except for a few grey hairs."

"Sunshine With Some Drizzle"
    Dr. Charleszetta Stalling

ACCIDENTLY ON PURPOSE

Plotted, I did to kill them. It would be an accident. I say accident because I really didn't want to kill them. It helped to justify the killing if they were accidently murdered. I didn't want to, I had to. I didn't want them messing up my pool, yard and sidewalk. It may sound selfish, but I don't like to step in mess. Therefore, I plotted how I would do it on purpose.

I searched and found the perfect dark charcoal rock. It was approximately eight inches long, five inches wide and three inches thick. It reminded me of death. That's what I would do. Kill them dead.

Gingerly, I lifted the large elephant leaf plant leaves, stepped under them and searched the ground for the pests. It took me a minute or so to find them. There they were hiding, three of them, all together touching each other. I looked around to make sure no one was watching me. I don't want to attract attention while I tried to accidently kill them on purpose. Slowly, I lifted my rock, as I took one last glance around. I slammed the rock down, with all of my might, on top of them, stepped on it and twisted it with my right foot to make sure. I don't want them to suffer. As a headstone, I left the rock in place.

Several days later, I heard the same annoying sound again. It was 7:30 AM. I am retired and don't like to get up until I wake up, usually 8:30 AM or so. Sure enough, with sleep and cracklings still in the corners of my eyes, I looked out my kitchen window. There was one in my pool and the other in the bushes by the pool. I knew the second one was there because I saw the leaves moving.

Quickly, I turned off my home alarm system, rushed outside, grabbed the long pool pole and tried to beat the daylights out of my unwelcome pests who seemed quite at home. The pests and my black and white feral cat looked at me like I was the crazy woman out of place. I screamed at the pests. They sat another ten seconds, squawked their disapproval and left.

"They will not get away with this!" I grabbed a rock and searched the bushes for several seconds. "Aha, I found you," I said with much satisfaction. There were only two of them. Again, I crushed them and left the rock as a headstone.

Three uneventful but pleasant days passed. Ah peace, it was so nice. On the fourth day, I was again, ruefully awaken at 7 AM. Can you believe that...7 AM? Generally, I don't feel like immediately getting up and screaming like a mad woman before I am fully awake.

I made coffee, drank it, and said my prayers then read my daily meditation.   After thanking God for his love and creation of all creatures, I armed myself with the kitchen broom.   Under the elephant leaves, I searched the ground for the pests.   "Oh, no!"   This time there were four of them snuggled next to each other.   They were beautiful, almost translucent white-white bigger than store bought AA eggs.

I was tired of accidently on purpose killing my pest's eggs. They were Mallard duck eggs.   The male Mallard had a colorful greenish-blue head with a white collar and his mate, the female was a motley brown and white.   They lived in this area before homes were built.

I collected the fresh Mallard eggs, put a rock in their place and placed the eggs in a basket before they could develop into chicks.

When my pool man came, I gave them to him and he gave them to his parents.   I don't know whether they were ever eaten or not.   What I do know is that I have not been able to eat an egg since I first killed them, accidently on purpose and that was two months ago.

GUILTY

Broadcast on television: Man pleads not guilty after driving with his wife on the hood of his car.

I started thinking. I wonder how it happened ? Perhaps, she fell on the car and he didn't know it. Perhaps, he was blind then he shouldn't drive.

The man was an airplane pilot driving 80 miles per hour with his wife as senior pilot, but he didn't know it.

He was taking her son. She grabbed the space for the disappearing wipers as her rope. Face down, she straddled the hood. Her inner thigh muscles stretched like riding a wide horse. He hoped he would hurt, but she rode with the help of her rope.

Now, he's facing trial for trying to: (1) pull her down from the skies; and (2) remove her from her thighs.

ALONE

I never told anyone this before. Rushing, I put on the finishing touches of my burgundy plum lipstick as I warmed up my car. I tilted my head back as I looked into the mirror between the sun visors.

What's that I see? I moved closer to the mirror. One long bright gray curled hair in my left nostril. I paused, turned off the engine and took time to look at the bright grey curled hair in my nose. How long had it been there? All alone and not noticed.

VITAMIN E

In May 2004, I had total knee replacement. My physical therapist suggested that I use vitamin E capsules instead of vitamin E oil in the bottle. The capsules were cheaper and just as effective in reducing scaring.

Faithfully, I used vitamin E oil from the capsules. I rubbed my knee gently in a circular pattern clock wise and counterclockwise for days, and eventually weeks.

After six weeks, I noticed a change. A new change. It was phenomenal. This was unusual for my knee. Never had I hair on my knee that I could see. Never had I shaved my legs. Now, I had a hairy knee. I stopped using vitamin E on my knee and placed it on my scalp.

SPEED HUMPS

Today I learned the difference between undulations and speed humps. Undulations consist of two consecutive humps. A speed hump is one hump.

Research has proved that one hump is just as effective as two humps. The one hump is more cost effective. Why not call them slow humps? After all, the humps do cause the driver to slow down.

EDGAR

Edgar was my unofficial adopted third stepfather. My mother and Edgar were together for approximately 15 years, never married but exchanged rings. As older folks, they shacked instead of getting married because it would have negatively affected their respective social security.

My brother, mother and I were Edgar's family because he had no other so he said. Therefore, we adopted him so to speak.

Edgar was a strong man who got up at five every morning. He was always making or fixing something until he developed gangrene in his big right toe.

We asked him what he wanted to do. He told us to make the decision. Whatever it was he would accept. We had his toe removed. He was never the same, lost his strength and seemed to slow way down. I went to see him every day.

Eventually, with tired eyes, he slowly stated, "I want to go home." We put the hospital bed by the front picture window in the living room. There he could look out, see life, children across the street running, laughing, playing, people getting in and out of cars, the lawn being cut that he used to mow weekly.

"This just isn't right," he sighted audibly. His frustration could be heard and seen. Another shallow sigh; he turned his head away from me. Edgar never complained though we could feel his pain. Once he became sick his time came sooner than expected. He gave his instructions to me:

This My Will to Live

Ease pain with medication
But, do not kill me
Just let me die peacefully
Don't prolong my life
Each sip one spoon of my blackberry wine

From a horizontal position on his back, we looked directly into each other's eyes as he slightly lifted his chin upward and struggled to release heartfelt words of "Thank... you." My eyes replied in kind as I held his hand and let my tears flow.

Edgar made his transition at 95 years young. He was a strong, hard-working, good man of few words who loved my mother and his adopted family.

After seven years, I can now put my feeling into words. "Edgar, your presence was my treasure!"

IN-BETWEEN AND CONFUSED

I ain't crazy. I need someone to talk to. It seems I'm here but not here. Going but not gone, in-between and confused.

Don't know where I am sometimes. I get confused and can't remember how to find the toilet or my bedroom. Another time, I put one cup of salt instead of sugar in my pie.

I go to sleep in the afternoon, wake up and think it is the next day. Some try to tell me it's the same day. I'm not stupid. I'm a big girl and know better. I get upset when people argue with me.

Yet, I move toward more unknown scenarios. Reluctantly, something or someone pulls me against my will not to be me as I am or think I am. Something doesn't seem quite right. I can't put my finger on it.

Like I said before, I'm not sure who I am sometimes, but I remember good...the pass like yesteryear is today for real. I remember in detail how I did the canning as a youngster 60 or 70 year ago. I canned string beans, tomatoes and even butter in glass jars that lasted for years. Candied pear preserve and grape jelly were my specialties.

Don't ask me what I had for breakfast, lunch or dinner today. I wasn't given any food today. I think they are trying to starve me. I haven't eaten in a while.

Did I tell you? Sometimes I repeat myself. Did I tell you that my two favorite pajama sets disappeared for a week? Then when I looked in my PJ drawer, there they were. I think somebody is coming into my house, using my things for a while then putting them back. My son has changed my door locks several times.

Sometimes I get so confused thinking about thinking, trying to get things straight, not remembering to remember, feeling useless, sick of being sick , I feel I'm spitting shit. Help me! I ain't crazy. I'm in-between and confused.

DON'T KNOW ABOUT HER

"She's ...different," I heard someone say.

Yes, I'm different. I am unique. I have a forward head, curious mind, bright dark brown eyes, smiling lips, slight curvature of the spine, round firm behind that sticks out, knocked knees and skinny legs that don't touch at the ankle. I carry all of it well. There is no other like me.

I look and act like I know where I am going. I hold my head high without being stuck up. I like what I like, whether you agree or even society. I know custom, eat with a fork and know how to deal with tack when I want. I may half agree with what you say or not at all. I obey my heart, thoughts. I don't imitate or wear the latest fashions. I create my own. I gotta be me. I can't hope, pray, or dare too much.

"Perhaps, she's dangerous," I heard someone say.

CHANGED

"I have changed, can't you see it?" I looked seriously into his eyes and upon his face. Verbally, I didn't respond. Internally, I responded, hopeful that he had changed. I didn't see anything different.

"I have found God!"

Fool, I thought, but didn't say. God wasn't lost! That's like saying Columbus discovered America where the Indians had lived for many, many years.

Now, when I think about it, perhaps, I should have laughed in his face, but I was hoping he had changed, too. I do now laugh at my own naiveté. Mind games, again.

Come to think of it, I do think he has changed... for the worse or either I'm just realizing it. Now I know he was always so.

WEIRD

On Wednesday, July 10, 2013, he looked thinner with his thin shaggy grey and white beard. His beard was now approximately four to five inches long. He didn't trim it, he affectionately patted it up with a cupped open hand. He showed me pictures of his passport; he looked much fatter in the face. He almost looked like someone else, maybe a brother, if he had one. Who knows?

"This is my old passport." He let me quickly look at it.

As I looked at it, I asked, "When did you come to the US?"

"About 1998."

"Here are the papers I need notarized." He reached for his passport as he handed me the papers.

"All you need do is sign right here in space number 9 and notarize in this box."

I unfolded the papers to see what they were about. I had not notarized such a document before.

"You just sign where it states, knows personally and for how long."

"Sunshine With Some Drizzle"
  Dr. Charleszetta Stalling

I continued to review the papers. "It says here that a birth certificate from your birth state needs to be shown. I also notice that your name here is different from the other passport."

"Yeah, I decided to change it and drop part of my name." He didn't say which part, but the name started with R, maybe Raphael or something as such.

"Do you have proof of name change? It further states that it should be signed by the magistrate or...."

"That's okay." He gathered his papers and put them neatly back into the manila envelope. "I had five papers, where is the other one?"

I shrugged, "I don't know, we have only sat here." He looked between the seats, behind my seat and finally between his seat and the side door. It had slid there.

"There's more than one way to skin a cat." I waited for more to be said.

It wasn't what he said or how he said it. It was more of what wasn't said. I felt tension, controlled anger. I looked at him in the dim lighted car with a questioning face, "What does that mean?" As I thought about it later, "What cat was he talking about? Did he mean it figuratively or what?"

"Sunshine With Some Drizzle"
   Dr. Charleszetta Stalling

~ 73 ~

"It's okay. I understand. I can get it done," he said with resolve.

"I am not familiar with this form. I'll check for information on the internet, tomorrow."

"Don't use my name!" He sounded somewhat alarmed to me.

"Why would I? I'll get basic information about passports."

"You know that anything you type, even when lost, stays for seven years. Anybody can get that information."

I fiddled with the radio to find a decent station and then turned it off in frustration. I was ready to go. This scene was getting very weird.

Meanwhile, he fiddled with his disposable camera he had taken out of his shirt pocket. "I hope this is still working." When I looked up, he pointed the camera in my direction.

"I don't want a picture taken." He tried to take one anyway.

"The light didn't flash," he exclaimed.

Was that suppose to make everything okay? "I got to go."

"Okay, Sweetie." I just hate that term, Sweetie or any such term that is not my name, especially when I don't know them well. Come to think of it. It didn't sound affectionate when he said it. It sounded like a putdown--which is a turn off to me. Doesn't matter. I won't be seeing him again. Why bother to tell him.

He played with his camera a bit more. The light came on this time. He pointed it in my direction again, but missed me.

"Bye." I leaned over and rolled up the window. He looked around and carefully checked to make sure he had all of his papers, got out the car and walked around to my side of the car.

"Roll the window down, so I can take your picture."

"See you later." Is this man crazy? What doesn't he understand and why is he so persistent about taking a picture of me?

He put the camera back up to his eye to take a picture. I turned the other way and left.

As I drove away, I glanced back to make certain that I was not being followed. Bye, bye.

MISTAKE CAPTURED

"I made a mistake," my son freely admitted-- softly as though talking with himself and thinking it through, again and again beating himself up.

As his mother, I could feel his unspoken broken spirit of guilt, heavy shame, and worry about his future, maintaining his good track record, no tickets, arrests or drugs; keeping his job and basically being an independent young man who could effectively take care of himself.

"I was the 'good' son who didn't get in trouble." His disappointment in self and shame was clearly heard. I felt his hurt.

After I figured out what I felt radiating from him, I put my thoughts into words and read them to him.

"That's exactly what I am feeling and thinking!"

"Son, we have power to control our thoughts and focus in life. Forgive yourself and ask God for forgiveness. Let's pray."

ALMOST GROWN

When I was fifty some odd years old, I went to my Mother to cry the blues. She listened quietly without comment. I ranted. I raved and talked about how unfair life is. I talked about my goodness, kindness and fairness. How I was hurt, disappointed and upset by His actions.

Mother listened quietly without comment. She didn't agree or disagree.

"What do you say and suggest, Mother?" I was seeking her wisdom and experience. There were several seconds of quiet.

"I won't say he's a dirty dog, but I will support you, once you make up your mind what you want to do. It's your life! Make your own decisions. Do what brings you peace and joy. Don't do anything you can't live with."